Contents

D1448517

1. Going up! 4

2. What if... I've got the wrong stuff? 8

3. What if... I get lost? 16

4. What if... I don't fit in? 25

5. What if... the older kids are horrible to me? ...35

6. What if... the teachers are scary? 50

7. What if... I can't do the work? (Part 1) 59

8. What if... I can't do the work? (Part 2) 72

9. What if... I get into trouble? 79

10. No worries! 89

1 Going up!

Going up to secondary school is like going on safari – it's a great adventure but sometimes, before you go, you can get a touch of the 'what ifs'.

Worries are a natural part of every new adventure. Some people handle them better than others, and some people hide them better, but everyone has them – and that's good because worries are nature's way of making you prepare.

What if I get bitten by a poisonous spider?

One way of preparing is by getting information

This book is full of information about going up to
secondary school. It covers all the most common
worries. If you're the sort of person who doesn't
like change, you might have quite a lot of worries.
If you love a challenge, you probably won't. If you're
a pessimist who always expects things to go wrong,
you might feel very worried, but if you're an optimist
your worries will probably be quite mild.

The particular things you might be worried about will also depend on what type of person you are, for instance:

- If you're a shy person, you might be worried about making new friends.
- If you haven't got much money, you might be worried about having the right stuff.
- If you've got big brothers and sisters, you probably won't be so bothered about bullying.
- If you're a whiz at map reading you won't have to worry about getting lost.

Going up to secondary school is a big step. Most secondary schools are huge; they have tons of teachers, busloads of bigger kids and weird rules you don't know anything about. If you're worried – don't worry! It's only natural.

Use your worries to show you what information you need. When you've got it, the worries will have served their purpose, and then they will just fade away.

Do the Quick Tick Quiz to see if this book can help.

Quick Tick Quiz

When I think about going up to secondary school,
I sometimes wonder (tick the relevant boxes)...

☐ **1**. What if I've got the wrong stuff?

☐ **2**. What if I get lost?

☐ **3**. What if the school cook puts poison in the chips?

☐ **4**. What if I don't fit in?

☐ **5**. What if pigs could fly?*

☐ **6**. What if the older kids are horrible to me?

☐ **7**. What if the teachers are scary?

☐ **8**. What if I can't do the work?

☐ **9**. What if someone crossed a
chicken with a cement mixer?**

☐ **10**. What if I get into trouble?

RESULTS

If you ticked number 3 – You've been watching too many scary movies - read on to get real.

If you ticked numbers 5 or 9 – you've got a short attention span but you like a laugh – read on for the jokes.

If you ticked any of numbers 1, 2, 4, 6, 7, 8 or 10 – you need some information. Read on!

*The price of bacon would go up. **They'd get a bricklayer.

2 What if... I've got the wrong stuff?

Obviously, when you go up to secondary school you want to look OK and not like a nerd. Well, then uniform is your friend! Almost all secondary schools have a uniform, and you can check out the details of yours on the school's website or in its brochure.

There are three things that aren't usually covered by uniform rules – coats, shoes and bags. Schools usually specify no boots or trainers but, beyond that, they just say these items should be 'sensible' or 'suitable'. Which isn't really a lot of help.

How to get the right coat, shoes and bag

Why are football stars so cool?
Because they've got lots of fans!

They've also got lots of money – unlike most kids at secondary school. You don't need to spend a fortune to fit in, but it's worth investing a bit of time in doing some research.

Big brothers and sisters – your own or somebody else's – can be a useful source of information. Notice what they wear to school. If you get on well with them, ask their advice. (This is probably not a good idea if you don't get on well.)

Do you think an army-style rucksack would be good?

Go and watch the big kids when they come out of school. Check out their choice of shoes, coats and bags – but be discreet! Take one of your mates and stand at a bus stop nearby as if you're waiting for a bus, or sit in a café on the high street, or go secondary-student-spotting in the local shopping centre. Ideally, do it a couple of times, in different weather conditions.

Sometimes parents get it into their heads that everyone at secondary school will be wearing 'sensible lace-ups'. If the kids at your secondary school aren't, take your parents secondary-student-spotting with you so that they can see for themselves.

KIT TIP

Remember that your parents have already had to cough up the cash for your uniform. Don't give them a hard time if they recoil at buying the most expensive trainers. When you've done the research, you'll see you don't need them, and they're probably against the rules anyway.

What's in the bag?

You can check out the best sort of bag by simply noticing what the big kids have – but what about the stuff that's inside the bag? On the first day, you'll just need a pencil

case, plus any items the school suggests, such as a pocket dictionary for the foreign language you'll be studying. You might also want to put in a snack, in case lunchtime at your new school is much later than you're used to. Your school might use a cashless system for lunch money, that your parents can top up online, but if there are any problems, you can always go along to the office – they'll make sure you don't go hungry.

Don't take more money than you need to for bus fares, etc. Most schools don't like students bringing in cartloads of cash! A lot of schools aren't keen on mobile phones either, and have strict rules about them, which usually include:

- Phones should not be seen or heard during the school day.
- Headphones should not be seen either. (It's hard trying to explain the human digestive system to someone who's blasting hip-hop.)
- Portable speakers – absolutely not!

Phones are rarely stolen at school but they can go missing, and if you lose yours, that will be your responsibility.

WATER **TIP**

If you take a bottle of water to school, make sure you screw the lid on properly. Research shows that 100% of students soak all the books in their bag at least once in the course of their school career.

The pencil case

You're going to need a good-sized pencil case because some or all of these things will have to fit into it (your new school will say on its website exactly what they want you to bring):

- pens
- pencils (plain and coloured)
- highlighters
- geometry set
- pocket calculator (even if you already know how many pockets you've got!)
- eraser (What did the eraser say to the pencil? 'Take me to your ruler...')
- ruler!

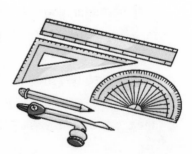

Once you've got everything...

Use permanent markers to write your name on all your clothes and equipment. This is essential with school uniform because everyone's lost property looks pretty much the same. It also means people are less likely to pinch your things.

The art of organisation

At secondary school, the day is usually divided into five or six subject sessions in different parts of the building. Some schools have lockers where you can leave things, but you don't always have time to get to your locker between lessons. Some schools don't have lockers at all, so you'll be walking miles each day, with all the books and equipment you need on your back. Obviously, you don't want to carry any more than you have to, unless you're training for a hike in the Himalayas. You will have to master the art of organisation.

Every evening before you go to bed, check your timetable to see what lessons you have the next day. Put all the textbooks, folders, PE equipment (not forgetting deodorant for afterwards) and other assorted stuff you need in your bag, and take out everything you don't need. It takes a bit of getting used to, but it isn't rocket science.

To see if you're going to have a problem with packing, try the packing puzzle.

The packing puzzle

Look at the timetable on the right, then use your skill and ingenuity to decide how many of the objects from the opposite page you will need to pack.

TIME	MONDAY
9:00AM	Tutor time
9:30AM	Lesson 1 – Maths
10:30AM	Lesson 2 – Geog
11:30AM	Break
12:00AM	Lesson 3 – Music
1:00PM	Lunch
2:00PM	Lesson 4 – English
3:00PM	Lesson 5 – PE

RESULTS

9: Spot on!* **Any other number:** Try again, and get your mum or dad to check it. (This is also a good idea if you aren't sure that you've got your real packing right.)

*So long as they're the right nine, of course – maths, geography, English and music books, wallet or purse, pencil case, calculator, PE kit and snack bar.

TICK TOCK TIP

If you like to wear a watch but it's
a) pure gold, encrusted with diamonds, or
b) got the Hulk/Peppa Pig/Barbie on it,
*   you might want to think about*
*   getting a different one for school.*

Like I said, getting the right stuff isn't rocket science. Now you just need to make sure you're in the right place at the right time. Do I hear you say, 'But what if I get lost?'

3 What if...
I get lost?

There are fewer secondary schools than primary schools, so it stands to reason that you'll probably have further to travel when you go up. If you're worried you might get lost on the way the best thing you can do is practise.

If you're planning to walk or go by bike, do a couple of dummy runs in the holidays. It's not at all scary, no matter what the bit of black tarmac says...

*Why was the bit of black tarmac scared of the bit of green tarmac?
Because he was a cycle path! (psychopath)
Sorry – that's awful!*

Go with a friend who lives nearby, or try to rope in your sister/brother/mum/dad to go with you. Do the same if you're planning to travel by bus. If you live in the countryside and you're going to be travelling on a school bus that doesn't run in the holidays, ask your parents to drive the route with you a few times.

When you're not worried any more about getting lost on the way to school, you can concentrate on worrying about getting lost once you arrive.

Compared with primary schools, most secondary schools are HUGE. They have great facilities, such as proper science labs, art rooms, IT suites, music studios, technology rooms, drama suites, sports halls and playing fields. They may also have enough classrooms for 1,000+ students. Fortunately, before you actually arrive, you'll have at least one taster day, which is a chance to meet your tutor, find your form room and have a good look around. Some secondary schools actually organise orienteering games and treasure hunts to help you learn where everything is.

On your first day, you'll probably be asked to assemble in the hall, or some other large, easy-to-find area, and there will be members of staff on hand to show you the way, in case you've forgotten.

TWO FIRST DAY **TIPS**

1. *Be on time.*
2. *Plan with a friend to either travel together or to meet up in the car park before you go in.*

So far, so good – you can't possibly get lost!

One of the first things your form tutor will do is give you a timetable and a map.

MAP **TIP**

If you want a sneak preview right now, there may well be a map on your secondary school's website. Take a look!

The school map

In most secondary schools, the classrooms are organised into subject areas. This is very helpful because you always know roughly which area you should be in for any particular lesson. To help you remember where they are, your form tutor may suggest you colour in the subject areas on your map, using a different colour for each one.

The most important room is your form room, because you will meet there every morning, and possibly afternoon, for registration before lessons.

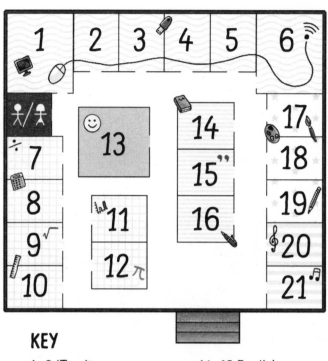

KEY

1–6 IT suites

7–12 Maths

13 Head Teacher

14–16 English

17–19 Art

20–21 Music

Some schools have one-way systems in corridors that get particularly busy, and your form tutor will show you where to mark these on your map. They will also show you where the Year 7 (or S1 if you go to school in Scotland) toilets are, as well as any special provisions for break times, such as designated Year 7 areas and homework rooms.

The wisdom of sheep

Sheep get a bad press for following each other around and sticking together, but they are actually a great role model for new kids at secondary school. (I don't know any good sheep jokes – only baa-d ones!)

It makes sense to stick with the crowd for the first few days when you're changing rooms after every lesson because:

🐑 At least one of you will probably have some idea about where you're supposed to be going.
🐑 If it all goes pear-shaped and you end up in a Year 10 art class, it will be much less embarrassing than if you were on your own.

Sticking with the crowd is very easy in the first year of secondary school because you do most of your lessons with the same form group. After morning registration, you'll all go off to maths together, for example, and from maths you'll all shoot off to the next lesson.

For the odd thing like sports, where you might be divided up, you'll still have lots of people from your own class to go with. The same goes for setting: your new school might divide you into sets in the first year – although that's not likely.

Two's company (three's even better)

When you're not walking between classes in a big group, it's still a good idea to get someone to go with you to things like lunchtime clubs or sports practices because you're less likely to get lost (two heads are better than one). Also, if you do get lost:

- You won't panic.
- It'll be easier to ask the way (you might be able to get your mate to do it!).
- Later on, you'll be able to have a laugh about it together.

You don't have to be best friends – you're just helping each other out. So be prepared to return the favour in the early days if someone else asks you.

Jo and Sasha's story

Jo was putting her things back in her bag after her first maths lesson when she dropped her pencil case on the floor. The pens and pencils went everywhere! Luckily for Jo, Sasha, who was sitting next to her, stopped to help her pick them up. By the time they had finished, everyone else had gone.

Their next lesson was in the IT suite. Jo and Sasha didn't know where that was, so they looked at the map and then set off... in the wrong direction. They ended up outside the sixth form common room, and had to ask a friendly sixth former the way.

By the time they got to the IT suite – ten minutes late – they were both in a bit of a panic. But they needn't have worried. 'Well done, you two,' the teacher said, as they walked into the empty room. 'You're the first ones to arrive. The rest of your class were last seen going the wrong way down the maths corridor!'

If the worst comes to the worst...

By using your map, sticking with the crowd and finding a few friends to hang around with, you should be able to avoid getting lost or at least getting lost on your own.

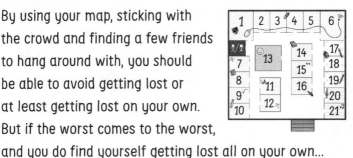

But if the worst comes to the worst, and you do find yourself getting lost all on your own...

First

Get things in perspective. Ask yourself, 'What's the worst thing that could happen?'

1. You might be a bit late for your next lesson.
2. Your teacher might be angry.
3. The other kids might laugh.

OK, so you're going to miss a few minutes of French, and Monsieur might tell you off – it's not exactly fatal, is it? It's not even very likely, as most teachers don't make a fuss about first years getting lost and turning up late – they're used to it. The other kids aren't likely to laugh at you, either, because they're all in the same boat. But if they do, why not laugh with them? (Discreetly, of course – you don't want to upset the teacher.)

23

Second

Ask for directions.

Don't be embarrassed. Some of the most famous explorers in the world have found themselves impressively lost, so it's nothing to be ashamed of.

Two top explorers
who got lost

David Livingstone
– He went looking for the source of the Nile, not realising he was actually going up the River Congo.

Christopher Columbus – *When he sighted America in 1492, he thought he was looking at India.*

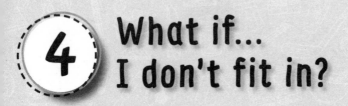

4 What if... I don't fit in?

By the time you've been right through primary school you know everybody in your year really, really well. You've been friends with everyone you could possibly be friends with and learnt to live with the rest.

Going up to secondary school means that, for the first time in years, you're starting again in a big group of people you don't know. You've got the chance to make lots of new friends. So does that mean you're going to lose the old ones? Not at all!

Some secondary schools try to put new students in the same class as their old friends from primary school. Quite often, you get to choose the people you would particularly like to be with (and the people you would particularly not like to be with, if you feel strongly about it).

Spread your net

You'll never have had the chance to meet so many people of your own age, so make the most of it. Spread your net! Meet people from other classes by:

- attending any social events organised by the school for new students
- getting involved in sports
- linking up at break times with old friends in different classes and meeting their new mates
- joining in with lunchtime clubs and activities.

Sam and Ayush's story

Sam and Ayush weren't sure which clubs they wanted to join when they went up to secondary school. Sam decided to try chess, football and creative writing. Ayush decided to leave it for a while, until he knew his way around a bit and was feeling more confident.

After a few weeks, Sam decided he didn't like chess so he just stopped going. Ayush decided he was ready to try chess and football, but by then the chess club was organised into a league and teams had been chosen for the football club.

Ayush realised, too late, that it was much easier to drop out after a few weeks than to join in after a few weeks. If only he had plucked up his courage earlier!

'But I'm just too shy/boring/geeky to make friends...'

Luckily, not everyone in the world is loud, confident and super-sociable. If they were, we'd all have to get ear plugs. Everyone's different, and everyone's got a different idea about what sort of friendships they want. Some people are happy with one best friend, and others want to be in the middle of a big group. Some people don't need any close friends at all, but like to be on the edge of several groups. Some people want a quiet, studious friend they can talk to and others want a big, rowdy gang to mess around with.

Making friends isn't about having any particular personality – it's about having good friendship skills. If you haven't got them already, you can easily learn them.

Check out whether you need to brush up on your friendship skills by doing the Friendliness Test.

Friendliness Test

1 When I pass someone I vaguely know...

A I smile.
B I blush and look at the floor.
C I say, 'What are you looking at, loser?'

2 When I meet someone new...

A They will probably like me (I'm a nice kind of person).
B I think they might like me (miracles can happen).
C They're not going to like me but what do I care?

3 When I talk about myself...

A I keep it positive.

B I like to share my problems (all the time!).

C I think it's important for everyone to know how clever/rich/beautiful/popular I am.

4 When I'm trying to get to know someone...

A I ask questions and listen to the answers.

B I don't ask questions because they might think I'm being nosy.

C I ask questions and then tell an amusing story about myself before they have a chance to answer.

5 When I want to join in with a new group...

A I join in but stay on the sidelines until I understand how the group works.

B I hang around at a distance and hope someone notices me.

C I get straight in there and take over.

6 In a discussion...

A I like hearing everyone else's opinion as well as having my say.

B I don't want to say anything in case people disagree with me.

C I don't think anyone should disagree with me because I'm basically always right.

7 If someone makes it clear they don't want to be friends with me...

A I go and find somebody else.

B I assume it means nobody will want to be friends with me.

C I hang around anyway (they're going to like me!)

RESULTS

If you got mostly As...
Skip the rest of this chapter and come round to my house for tea!

If you got mostly Bs...
Your heart's in the right place but you're not the easiest person to get to know. Work on boosting your confidence so you can have more fun.

If you got mostly Cs...
The bad news is, you need help! The good news is, it's right here.

How to boost your friendship skills

If you got all Bs and Cs in the Friendliness Test, don't beat yourself up about it. While the A students have been concentrating on their social lives, you've probably been busy developing other skills that they're not very good at, like investigating astrophysics or knowing everything there is to know about the Premiership.

Build up your friendship skills now by taking a leaf out of their book. Read back over the quiz and see how the A's do it. You'll notice there are seven questions, and each of them reveals one of the secrets of likeable people.

The seven secrets of likeable people

1) They smile!

It's a scientific fact that when you smile, people are inclined to like you. Saying 'hi' is an optional extra, but basically, why not? The worst thing that could happen is that the person might blank you, and that's

   a) not likely

   b) not fatal.

2 They expect other people to like them.
Expecting people not to like you is actually a way of
rejecting their friendship.

3 They are interesting, because they can talk
about themselves without boasting or grumbling
all the time.

TALKING **TIP**

Confidence is a good thing, but if you don't want to sound
judgemental or boastful, express yourself in terms of how
you feel. For example, 'I love football' sounds better than,
'I'm brilliant at football'. 'I found Level 7 hard' sounds
better than 'What – you're only on Level 7?!'

4 They are interested in other people.

5 They know the difference between joining in
and taking over.

6 They enjoy the fact that everyone is different.

7 They understand that even though they're
doing all the right things, not everyone will want to
be friends with them. They don't take it personally.

Going for gold

The seven secrets of likeable people are the gold standard – they're what to aim for, though everyone falls short of them sometimes. So don't feel defeated if you mess up. Keep trying!

I look like my mum – she's a model.

Practice makes perfect, and here's a bit of practical work you can do to build up your skills. Start right away!

Being likeable – the daily practice

1. Cut seven small pieces of paper.
2. Write one of the phrases below on each piece.
3. Fold the pieces of paper and jumble them up.
4. Pick one out every morning.

Smile

Look people in the eye when you talk to them

Pay a compliment

Say hi

Ask a question and really listen to the answer

Say something positive about yourself

Help someone

Think about it throughout the day. Try to do what it says at least once more than you normally would during the day.

Some people think that being nice is for losers, but don't let them put you off. Research shows that doing a good deed every day makes people feel happier than anything else – including having more money. That's a fact!

It isn't difficult to make new friends at secondary school because everyone in your year is like you – dead keen to make new friends. If you brush up on your friendship skills and remember the seven secrets of likeable people you'll find it even easier.

5 What if... the older kids are horrible to me?

At primary school, you're used to being the biggest fish in a little pond; at secondary school you'll be the smallest fish in a huge one. It isn't a comfortable thought! But the thing to remember about older kids is:

What's your problem?

They are just the same as you, except a couple of years older.

Here's Jason. He's in Year 10. He looks pretty scary, doesn't he?

Now let's see what's going on inside his head...

I hope there are some chips left at lunchtime.

Did I leave my Geography book at home?

That Jodie's well fit!

I wish Ethan would stop messaging me.

Do hedgehogs have ears?

Bigger doesn't mean nastier and, in fact, as people mature they usually sweeten up like a plum. By the time Jason is in the sixth form for example, he may look like a great hairy giant and be covered in tattoos and piercings, but he'll be as nice as pie inside because most sixth-formers are.

 ## A note about sixth forms...

Not all secondary schools have a sixth form. What a pity! Sixth-formers emerge from school uniform like butterflies coming out of a cocoon. They brighten up the place, and sometimes have extremely interesting dress sense!

Of course, when you first arrive at secondary school you probably won't see much of the sixth-formers because they'll all be too busy drinking coffee in their common room. Your arrival won't make much difference to them but it will make a big difference to the kids who are just a bit older than you. When you arrive, they'll be making a transition just like you, only instead of becoming the youngest kids in school, they're becoming not-the-youngest. Just as you might feel suddenly smaller, they will feel suddenly bigger.

Feeling bigger means they will:

- be willing to help you and show you the ropes
- make jokey remarks (the brighter ones)
- welcome you in sillier ways (the immature ones).

Willing to help

There's nothing quite so satisfying as knowing stuff and passing it on to someone else who doesn't. It gives you a warm glow, like any other generous act, and it makes you feel mature and efficient.

Imagine this: in primary school, the new Reception kids have just started and you see one crying in the corridor because he can't find his classroom.

What do you feel like doing? Laughing and running off? I don't think so. You're going to show him the way, because:

  a) that solves his problem

  b) it makes you feel good about yourself.

Helping is human nature, and although some Year 8s and Year 9s might not look all that human, they are.

Jokey remarks

Everybody who starts a new job or goes into a new school is likely to have to put up with jokey remarks.

At your new school, for example, they've probably got a pet name for Year 7s, such as 'maggots'. 'Hello, maggots!' they might say, when they pass you and your friends in the corridor. They'll have stories about various horrible (and completely imaginary) initiations that new kids have to go through – stories which almost always

 involve the 'head', 'toilet' and 'flush'. They'll also make dark hints about teachers you haven't met yet – 'You've got Mr Williams for science? Bad luck!'

It's a bit tedious, but don't worry – they'll soon get it out of their system.

Sillier welcomes

Sillier ways of welcoming you will usually refer to your size. The older kids might pat you on the head, for example, as if to say, 'Aren't you sweet?' and 'Aren't you smaller than me!' They might put their bag on your head (same message). This can occasionally seem scary, but it's usually quite good-natured. Take it with good humour, and don't get your knickers in a knot. If you've got some hairy great Year 9 patting you on the head, remember the ancient wisdom of 'Knock, knock'...

> *Knock, knock*
> *Who's there?*
> *Boo!*
> *Boo who?*
> *There's no need to cry – it's only a joke!*

You may not appreciate being patronised by the bigger kids, but on the whole it won't be malicious.

Now pay attention, because I'm going to tell you the secret of keeping it that way.

The secret of keeping it sweet

*How can you tell that owls
are cleverer than chickens?
Have you ever heard of Kentucky Fried Owl?*

Chickens aren't famous for their brainpower, but there is one really important thing they know, and that is how pecking order works.

Pecking order

When you introduce a new chicken into a flock, the first thing that happens is the other chickens jump on her and give her a pecking. It isn't a good idea to try to stop them, and anyway there's no point because it all blows over very quickly. Besides, they're only going through the motions; they don't actually hurt her.

As soon as the other chickens have shown the new one they're the boss, and she's accepted this by not taking them on, they all get along fine. The new chicken has to watch her step for a while, and not try to muscle in when the corn arrives, for instance, or pinch the best perch, but she won't have any more trouble. Pretty soon, she'll just be one of the gang, and the others won't even remember she's a newcomer. (Chickens are not famous for their memories either!)

As long as you accept that the big kids rule the roost for the time being, you'll be fine. But I have it on good authority (Ally, Year 9) that 'Nobody likes a cocky Year 7'. Do the Attitude Test to see if you've got the makings of a cocky Year 7.

 ## Attitude Test

1 A big kid wants to get to her locker and you're leaning on it. Do you:

A Scuttle off and hide.
B Refuse to budge.
C Move out of the way.

2 You see some Year 11s gossiping beside your locker. Do you:

A Decide you don't need your PE kit after all.

B Eavesdrop and then loudly offer your opinions on the matter.

C Get your PE kit and leave.

3 It's registration time but there's a Year 10 you don't like the look of standing in the doorway of your form room. Do you:

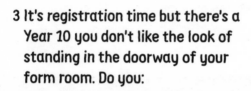

A Go and cry in a cupboard.

B Tell him to shift his carcass.

C Slip past without making a fuss.

4 You're five minutes late for art because you can't find the art room. You want to ask a group of big girls the way. Do you:

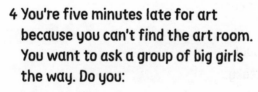

A Say nothing (they look too scary!).

B Demand, 'Hey, you! Where's the art room?'

C Ask nicely, 'Could you tell me the way to the art room?'

5 Some sixth-formers are crossing the playground. One of them is wearing a bright green waistcoat and yellow-tinted shades. Do you:

A Run and hide.

B Point and stare.

C Secretly admire his nerve (but probably not his dress sense!).

RESULTS

Mostly As – On the up-side, the bigger kids probably won't even notice you. On the down-side, neither will anyone else.

Any Bs at all – You are too cocky by half. Good luck – you might need it!

Mostly Cs – Well done. Top marks!

If you're very funny or you've got big brothers and sisters in the school, you might be able to get away with being a bit cocky, but otherwise:

- Don't act tough.
- Don't be cheeky.
- Don't try to be cool.

Trying to impress the bigger kids by posing, swearing, being rude or carrying out acts of petty vandalism such as blocking up the sinks in the loos will just mean you're going to get laughed at.

It's actually quite comfortable being at the bottom of the pecking order because you don't have to puff yourself up and make an impression. You can just watch and learn. So don't fight it. Enjoy it! Before you know it, the new Year 7s will be watching and learning from you.

But what about bullying?

When you first go up to secondary school you may well have to put up with some banter, and if you get too big for your boots the older kids might not like it. But with all those big kids around, should you be worried about bullying?

All schools have a minority of pupils who think it's OK to taunt, abuse, intimidate and attack other people, but all schools also have strategies for dealing with them. You can check out your new school's anti-bullying policy on its website.

If you have a problem with bullying, tell one of your teachers – they're not really scary, as you will see in the next chapter. If that teacher doesn't sort it out, tell another one. There are loads of them!

Fatema's story

Fatema was opening her packed lunch when some boys in her year came up and pinched her crisps.

Fatema told the lunchtime supervisor... but she said, 'I wouldn't worry about it. You're not exactly fading away, are you?'

Fatema was (understandably) very annoyed. She told her form tutor what had happened. He spoke to the boys and made them apologise. They didn't do it again. A few weeks later, the lunchtime supervisor left. The rumour was that she had got the sack, because it turned out that lots of other people had complained about her, besides Fatema.

Secondary schools are good at sorting out physical bullying because it's easy to identify and prove. Things like hitting people and stealing their stuff are also against the law, and they have a legal duty to protect you.

It's a fact!

In a major Childline survey, the majority of kids who complained to teachers about physical bullying said that it was quickly sorted out.

Sometimes schools are also good at dealing with verbal bullying and teasing, but that's much harder. Even if the teachers can't completely prevent it, you can always talk to them about it. Many schools have befriending schemes, so there will be older kids who are there to help you too.

If you have a problem with teasing that your teachers can't sort out, it's a good idea to learn some psychological self-defence skills. You may not be able to stop people being mean to you, but you can stop it undermining your self-confidence and making you miserable. To find out how, read *Bullies, Bigmouths and So-Called Friends*, by me. It's really good!

Teasing can be a drag but it doesn't have to wreck your life. In fact, a lot of famous, successful people say they got their mental toughness from learning to cope with being teased at school.

Seven super successful people who were bullied at school

1. Lady Gaga, singing superstar
2. Barack Obama, 44th US president
3. Victoria Beckham, fashion designer
4. Prince Harry, top royal
5. Sir Ranulph Fiennes, ace explorer
6. Jennifer Lawrence, movie star
7. Tom Daley, Olympic diving champion

When it comes to cyberbullying, that actually happens less than you might think, because everything is traceable, so it's virtually impossible to get away with it. If you get a message that upsets you:

- Don't respond.
- Block the person.
- Keep the message for evidence.
- Tell an adult.

Schools have clear policies and are used to dealing with this kind of problem. General information on how to manage your social media and messaging will be covered in lessons.

How not to be a cyberbully

It can be much easier to say hurtful things online than to a person's face, so be careful.

- *Think before you post a message. If you wouldn't say it in person, don't send it.*
- *Don't take or share photos or videos that other people might find embarrassing – you wouldn't like it if they did it to you. (Also, it's illegal to share people's images without their permission – you have been warned!)*

For more information on bullying, check out these websites:

www.childline.org.uk
www.bullying.co.uk
www.anti-bullyingalliance.org.uk

Now forget bullying!

You are bound to feel a bit worried about bullying when you first go up to secondary school, but that's just nature's way of keeping you safe. Whenever you are moving into a new environment it's a good idea to be slightly cautious and get the lie of the land first, before you start throwing your weight around.

The likelihood of being physically bullied is very small, and although verbal bullying is more common, you can learn to handle it and you can always talk to teachers. So if you feel really, really, really worried it probably just means that either you've got an over-active imagination or someone else has and they've been telling you stories.

Remember that the bigger kids are just like you, and bear in mind the secret of keeping things sweet. Then you won't draw attention to yourself in a negative way, and you're unlikely to fall foul of bullies. You're much more likely to find that the older kids just want to help you out!

6 What if... the teachers are scary?

The only thing that's scary about secondary school teachers is that there are just so many of them! At primary school, you have one teacher per year, and by the time you've reached the top class you know them all pretty well. But at secondary school, you can have 15 or more teachers a year.

When you add all the classroom assistants, librarians, lab technicians and other assorted support staff, you might start to wonder – 'How on earth am I going to get to know who's who?' The answer is, very gradually! But don't worry about it, because the only ones who really matter to you are (in order of importance):

- your form tutor
- your head of year
- your subject teachers.

Your form tutor

 First year form tutors are generally selected for their niceness (head teachers save their mean, sarky types for the rowdy Year 10s). You will probably see your form tutor once a day for morning registration in your form room. This means your form tutor gets to know you pretty well, and you get to know him/her too.

Your form tutor might not teach you at all, but they are like a primary school class teacher in that:

- They're the first person to talk to if you have any problems.
- They're the person your parents need to write to if they have any concerns, or need to take you out of school for dental appointments, etc.
- They're the person that other kids and teachers will talk to if they have a problem with you.

Sometimes, your form tutor might not be able to sort things out, or perhaps the problem you have is actually with them. At primary school, you'd have gone to see the headteacher. At secondary school, you go to see your head of year.

Your head of year

Most secondary schools are so big that the headteacher and their deputies occupy misty heights where mere mortals rarely go.

HEADTEACHER

DEPUTY HEAD

DEPUTY HEAD

YEAR HEAD

YEAR HEAD

YEAR HEAD

YEAR HEAD

FORM TUTOR

FORM TUTOR

FORM TUTOR

FORM TUTOR

FORM TUTOR

You might sometimes have assemblies with the head or deputy head, but your regular weekly assembly will probably be taken by your head of year. They will soon get to know you all, the same way as your head teacher did at primary school.

Your head of year will already know a bit about you before you start, because they will have been in contact with your old school. They will also know how you are getting on with your work, through talking to your subject teachers.

Subject teachers

The great thing about having loads of different subject teachers is – **they're all different!** That makes life really interesting and varied.

The tricky thing about having loads of different subject teachers is – **they're all different!** That means it's going to take you a while to get to know their funny little ways.

Just because Mr Easy-Osy, your English teacher, isn't too bothered that you forgot to do your homework, it doesn't mean that Mrs Motivator, your maths teacher, won't make you do double tonight.

And just because Ms Madd finds your plastic dog poo hilarious, it doesn't mean that Mr Mardy will. One teacher's idea of having a laugh might be another teacher's idea of being cheeky.

Look at the picture and guess what happens next...

The point is, you don't know, because you don't know the teacher. Until you've got the measure of your teachers, why not sit back and learn from other people's mistakes? Build up your credit by being polite, doing your homework and contributing in class – it's a well-known fact that people who are popular with the teachers get away with a lot more than disruptive kids. It's a win-win situation!

Your subject teachers see hundreds of different kids a week, so they'll take a while to get to know you. People with older siblings in the school tend to be noticed first, especially if they have

an unusual surname. Don't be jealous of them though, because that isn't always an advantage. Some people who have super brilliant or super troublesome big siblings might actually wish they weren't at the same school.

As you all get to know each other, you'll probably get along fine because kids and teachers usually do. So I'll keep the problems section brief...

Two possible problems

 'I don't like one of my teachers'

First – look on the bright side. At secondary school, you only have to put up with teachers you don't like for a few hours a week max.

Next – focus on the good. Try this experiment...

What happens when you focus on the good...

Go through a whole lesson noticing all the things you don't like about the teacher – she acts like she's one of us, she gossips with the cool girls, etc.

How does your body feel?
What are you thinking?

Now go through a whole lesson noticing all the good things about the teacher – she knows a lot about her subject, she didn't bite my head off because I forgot my book, etc.

How does your body feel?
What are you thinking?

RESULTS

I'm not going to tell you – find out for yourself!

The most surprising thing about this experiment, for a lot of people, is that it makes you notice that you can choose what you think about other people. You can like most people if you focus on their good points.

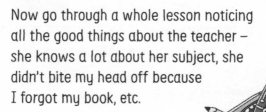

(2) 'One of my teachers doesn't like me'

First – test your idea. Ask yourself:

- Could I be imagining it?
- Am I being over-sensitive?

If the answer is no, ask yourself:

- Am I doing something to annoy them? (Be honest!)
- Am I not doing something they want me to do,
  e.g. homework, paying attention in class?

If the answer is yes – sort it! If the answer is no, it might be worth having a talk with the teacher/ your form tutor/your head of year. Bad relationships between students and teachers are usually the result of misunderstandings, and the best way to clear those up is by communicating.

At secondary school you have to learn how to get along with lots of different teachers, and that's exciting. If you have any problems, your form tutor and head of year are always there to help you sort them out.

Felix's story

Felix couldn't do anything right for his RE teacher. It came to be the class joke that she was always telling him off. She would have a go about his bad attitude, and everyone would laugh behind their hands.

Felix went to see his head of year. He explained that he was unhappy because his RE teacher seemed to hate him, and he didn't understand why.

Felix's head of year invited the RE teacher to join them. She said she felt that Felix was a ring-leader, encouraging the other kids to laugh at her. She had indeed come to regard him as a problem. Felix said he felt she always had it in for him, and that didn't feel fair.

They decided that it would be best if she avoided telling him off in class, and he avoided giving her any reason to. Then there was nothing for the other kids to snicker about, and Felix and his teacher had the satisfaction of having sorted things out in an adult, cooperative way.

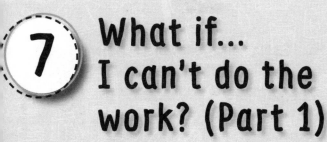

7 What if...
I can't do the
work? (Part 1)

At secondary school, the curriculum is organised in a different way from primary school. You have a different teacher for each subject and a few new subjects as well just for luck. The thing to remember about new subjects such as physics and French is that most of the other kids haven't done them before, either.

Just because the curriculum is organised differently, that doesn't mean it's harder. In fact, it should follow on quite smoothly from the work you were doing at primary school, because of primary-secondary links.

Primary-secondary links

Primary and secondary schools co-operate with each other in trying to make the move easier for you.

They often organise:

- induction days
- social and sporting events
- visits by secondary teachers and students who can answer any questions you might have
- summer schools
- taster lessons by visiting teachers.

That's the visible side of primary-secondary links – but there's more going on behind the scenes. Your primary school will have given up-to-date information to your new head of year about all the work your class has done so far and your own individual progress as a student.

Your new teachers will probably have seen your last primary school report, as well as your test results and samples of your work, which means that they can basically pitch their lessons at just the right level for you.

Of course, there may still be occasions when you feel either bored because the work's too easy, or confused because it's too hard. But if that happens, lots of other kids in your class will be in the same situation. Teachers are trained to spot problems and sort them out, but if yours don't, try to talk to them about it.

What about homework?

You are definitely going to
have more homework. You'll
probably have two or three
pieces of work a night,
which should take from an
hour to an hour and a half

to complete altogether. I say 'should' because
that's the theory.

In practice, of course, you have to decide for yourself
how long you're going to take over it. Some kids might
spend three or four hours over the homework tasks
that others will zip through in under an hour.

Make homework work for you

If you let homework take over your life...

- You'll start feeling stressed and unhappy.
- You'll have health problems such as sleeplessness,
  headaches and exhaustion.
- You won't have time for hobbies and sports.
- You'll have less time to spend with your mates.
- Your family life will suffer because:
  - you won't have time to slob around watching
    Netflix or playing online games

61

○ you'll hate everyone who does have time to
  slob around
○ your dad will give you grief for going to bed
  too late.

But if you just ignore homework and hope it'll go away...

● You'll fall behind with your work
● You'll get stressed out because you can't keep up
● Your teachers will be on your case all the time
● It'll always be in the back of your mind.

So you really have to learn how to handle it.

Five hot hints on handling homework

(1) Be positive!

Some people really enjoy homework but that doesn't go for everyone. Homework is a fact of life – it's a 'like it or lump it' situation. You can't avoid it, but you can choose whether you want to grumble and complain, or accept it and try to see what's good about it. As grumbling and complaining makes you unhappy and drives everyone else nuts, it's better to make the best of it.

Tell yourself that homework (I prefer to call it home learning) is a fabulous opportunity to learn new things in your own time and way. (It's worth a try!)

If that seems a bit airy-fairy, check out these rock-solid advantages of doing homework:

- It's definitely linked to better test grades.
- You can use it to get your parents to take you to great places like castles, animal sanctuaries, museums, the seaside... all in the name of research.
- You couldn't cover everything in the curriculum without it.

● It's a handy excuse for getting out of things you don't want to do, such as washing up.

● It also means you can chat to your mates for hours without too much hassle from your mum and dad if they think you're checking what you've got to do for homework.

(2) Use your resources

Make homework easier and more interesting for yourself by bumping up your knowledge of the subject. Ask your mum/dad/gran/uncle Sidney/big brother/big sister's nerdy boyfriend what they know about it. See what you can find online.

Any information you can find yourself has the added bonus of making your homework more interesting for your teacher to mark – and that's going to earn you a good grade.

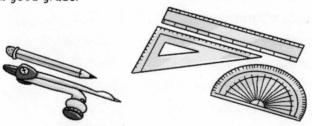

3 Organise

You might prefer to do a little bit of homework every night, or a couple of longer sessions several times a week, but the golden rule is this – never leave anything until the last minute. If you do, you might miss out on more fun things.

Imagine your mates decide to go bowling on a Tuesday night, for instance, and you've got geography homework due in on Wednesday. If you've done it in advance, you're free to go. If you've left it till the last minute, you aren't. Your teachers should help you by not setting homework that has to be handed in the next day.

As soon as you get home from school, check your homework diary or app. Plan which nights you are going to do it. It helps to set aside a particular time for homework, so that it just becomes routine. A lot of schools have homework clubs at lunchtime or after school.

(4) Decide what's most important

Parents and teachers say, 'Always do your best,' but they don't mean that literally. If you have a list of homework chores and you do your very best in all of them you're going to be up all night! You need to decide what's most important.

Some homework is interesting and useful, but some of it isn't. If you love colouring in (or you want to get out of tidying your room) then spend two hours creating an immaculate poster by all means.

But if you don't, there's not much learning value in it, so don't spend hours doing what's not important. On the other hand, fact-finding, reading, writing essays, revising for a test – they're all homework tasks that will enhance your learning, and are worth the effort.

Sometimes, you may have to decide what's important between homework and other things. There will be occasions when you'd be mad to give up a special opportunity in order to get your homework done. What if your uncle Bruce turned up unexpectedly for a flying visit from Australia? (However, these occasions should be few and far between!)

Use your common sense to decide when it's better to put your homework on hold. Tell the truth if your teacher's a reasonable type; that's usually better than thinking up an excuse.

If you do need an excuse, there are several tried-and-tested ones that every teacher has heard billions of times before. These could be safest, because generations of teachers have already been worn down by them.

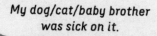

Five tried-and-tested homework excuses

My rabbit/hamster/ baby sister ate it.

My dog/cat/baby brother was sick on it.

I left it on the bus/ train/kitchen table.

Gemma/Andy/David borrowed my book and didn't give it back in time.

'Psycho' Simpson put it down the toilet.

Alternatively, you can think up your own original excuse, but only if your teacher has a good sense of humour.

Five original excuses

The doctor says I've developed an allergy to maths/English/food technology...

I read in the Daily Outrage that writing causes knuckle-fatigue

It was so fascinating finding out about the flood plains of Outer Wherever/the effects of oxygen starvation on the human body/the French words for various bits of furniture that I completely forgot I was supposed to be writing an essay on the subject.

Aliens landed in our garden and I spent the evening hiding in the cupboard under the stairs.

I bumped my head and got amnesia. (Homework... what homework?)

5 Don't get hung up on grades

Taking risks and making mistakes is part of the learning process. If you play it safe all the time you can miss the chance to extend yourself by trying new approaches and experimenting. Be happy with a mixture of grades because sometimes a low grade can mean you have had the courage to try something new and a high grade can mean you were playing safe.

The important thing about homework is to give it a go. Even if you get stuck, or don't think you've done a great job, your teacher will see that you have tried. Remember that any grade is better than no grade at all.

AN EXAMPLE

Sara's story

Sara always got top grades for her geography homework, and she spent hours every week trying to make sure that it was perfect. Most of the time, this just involved copying out of the book.

One day, the homework was drawing a map of the local area. Sara printed out a street plan that she found online and tried to copy it, but it was very complicated and it just kept going wrong. The more she worked on it, the messier it got. Eventually, she had to give up.

By then, it was getting late, but Sara wanted to have something to hand in. So she drew a quick map from memory, filling in the gaps where she wasn't sure what to put with sketches of things like the church and the corner shop.

Result: She still got top grades – for originality!

Note for non-academic types – don't undervalue your own strengths just because they may not be graded in school. It isn't always good to be a brainbox. Supposing you were stranded on a beach with the tide coming in and you needed someone to run for help – would you rather have Albert Einstein at the top of the cliff, or someone from your sports team? Or supposing you were upset because your hamster had died – would you rather have Charles Darwin explaining the biology, or the vet's nice nurse finding you a tissue?

8 What if... I can't do the work? (Part 2)

The work isn't harder at secondary school, but you do have to do more work at home.

The challenge is to get the work-life balance right. School work is important, but so is going out on your bike and giving the dog a bath.

See if you can strike a happy medium by doing the Quiz below.

IT CAME FROM PLANET ZARG

IN CINEMAS NOW

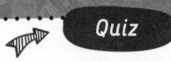

Quiz

1 Your mates are going to see 'It Came from Planet Zarg' at the cinema but you haven't finished colouring in your Black Death poster. Do you:

A See the film and forget the homework.
B Spend the evening getting your poster perfect.
C Finish it quickly and go to the film.

2 It's 9:30PM and you want to try out your new purple hair wax but your maths homework is due in tomorrow. Do you:

A Do the wax.

B Chuck the wax in the bin and do the maths.

C Do the maths and promise yourself you'll do the wax tomorrow.

3 Your grandpa's had a hang-gliding accident and your dad's going to visit him, but you have to write up a science report for tomorrow. Do you:

A Go and see your grandpa (anything to get out of science homework!).

B Do the science report and phone your grandpa.

C Go and see your grandpa (he was great when you had your appendix out).

4 You've got food tech in the morning and you forgot to buy the ingredients. You find everything in the cupboard except apricot jam. Do you:

A Forget about it and pinch some apricot jam off your mates in the lesson.

B Take the bus into town and go to the fancy food shop on the high street.

C Nip down to the corner shop (they've only got strawberry, but who's going to notice?).

5 You've been away for the weekend and now you've got five homework tasks to do by tomorrow. Do you:

A Pretend to be ill and take the day off school.
B Do everything on the list to the best of your ability (and get to bed at 4:00AM).
C Print off a picture for your geography poster and write some labels on it; do half your maths (to show you understand it); do stick men instead of your usual brilliant cartoons for your English storyboard; leave your copying-out-in-neat science (and explain why you didn't have time); leave your art collage (and tell your teacher you didn't want to rush it, so you need a bit more time).

6 You're not sure what you're supposed to be doing for French homework. Do you:

A Chat with your best friend for a few hours and then watch the show she was raving about.
B Fret for an hour. Ask a friend. Fret a bit more. Ask another friend, to check what the first one said. Make a group chat. End up not starting until 9:30PM and then get to bed really late.
C Phone a friend, talk about the homework and ask her round in an hour, because you'll have finished it by then.

Top tips for slackers

'All work and no play makes Jack a dull boy', as they say, but all play and no work means Jack's going to get very bored at school.

- Make yourself a good work space, maybe in your bedroom or on the floor beside the dog's basket. Choose somewhere you can have background music, if it helps. (Studies show that having classical music on in the background can help you to concentrate and work better. A lot of people find that any music is better than none.)
- Give yourself incentives ('I'll do half an hour of history and then watch TV/check the football score/ have a cup of hot chocolate...').
- Be realistic – accept that you've got to do some homework, because otherwise you'll soon fall behind.

Top tips for swots

You can work 24/7 and not be a workaholic, as long as you really love what you do. Some people are born geeks and that's great. If you are, don't fight it – enjoy!

But if you find that homework's taking over your life:

- Get a clock! Before you start a piece of homework say to yourself, 'Wherever I'm up to in half an hour, I'll stop.' This focuses the mind and helps you to complete the task in the set time.
- Get a life! Develop new interests and hobbies. Don't neglect your friends or give up things you love doing, like playing in a sports team.
- Let go of the need to be perfect.

Top tips for everyone

Whether you're learning at school or at home, it's much easier if you keep your brain in tip-top condition. Use these four brilliant brain boosters every day:

1 Exercise

A bit of exercise makes you healthier, happier (because it boosts the happiness chemicals in your brain)... and brainier! You don't have to be an athletics star or anything – just run up and down the stairs a few times, walk to school, kick a ball around...

2 Water

Dried-up brains don't work very well – that's a fact. So drink a large glass of water when you wake up, and try to drink some more during the day.

Note: Only water has this beneficial effect – not tea, coffee or fizzy drinks. Unlucky!

3 Screen-free time

Being glued to phone/computer/TV screens all day is bad for your body and brain – give your brain a break!

Switch off and take the dog for a walk, read a book, play on your keyboard, do some painting or drawing, write in your diary, learn to knit... Find things you enjoy so much that you completely forget about your phone for a while.

4 Breakfast

Brains need breakfast! People who skip breakfast are much more likely to have accidents, argue, fail tests and feel confused than those who don't.

It doesn't have to be a full fry-up or anything – most people would find that a bit challenging!

👍 👍 **Here are some great ideas for breakfast:**
- unsweetened cereal or muesli
- toast or bread with your favourite spread
- porridge
- fruit
- milk

- plain biscuits or crackers with cheese or cold meat (very popular in other parts of Europe)
- eggs (scrambled are very easy – ask your parents to show you how to cook them).

👍 **Here are some OK ideas:**
- sweet cereal
- chocky bickies
- milkshake/hot chocolate
- breakfast bars.

👎 👎 👎 **Here is the worst idea:**
- nothing.

Actually, don't skip any meals if you can help it. It's no good trying to write on an empty stomach – it's much better to write on paper!

9 What if...
I get into trouble?

> *What's the most unfortunate letter in the alphabet? U – because whenever there's trouble, u's right in the middle of it!*

Sometimes new kids worry that they might get into trouble by mistake because they don't know the rules. However, secondary school rules are as easy as ABC.

The ABC of school rules

(A) You can't do anything illegal.
That's stuff like theft or damage to property, physical assault, threatening behaviour, drug abuse, racial harassment (or any kind of discrimination) and bunking off.

(B) You can't do anything antisocial.
For example, bullying, littering, using bad language, smoking.

C **You can't do anything disruptive.**
That's things that make it hard for kids and teachers
to get on with their work, such as chatting all the time,
using phones in class or throwing things around.

If you're the kind of person who doesn't like being
bashed up, ploughing through piles of old crisp packets
or listening to some loudmouth kid at the back instead
of Mr Incredibly Interesting, the ABC of school rules will
already be second nature to you and you won't have
any problem sticking to them. The ABC of school rules
are just normal behaviour for most people – but what
about the D and E?

The D and E of school rules

D **You must do all your homework and
give it in on time.**

E **You must wear school uniform, as laid
down in the regulations.**

Homework and uniform rules are pretty straightforward,
but you might find them harder to stick to because they
can seem a bit random.

You might think, 'What's the point in copying out five pages of German spellings, when I can always just look them up?' and 'What harm am I doing to anyone by wearing pink ankle socks?'

Sticking to the rules

When rules don't seem important, it can be tempting to try to bend them a bit.

However, it's not usually worth the hassle because:

- Your teachers get fed up with telling you off
- Your classmates don't see why you should be winging it when they have to stick to the rules
- You'll only end up in detention.

Do the Skool Roolz Quiz – see if you can stick to the rules and keep out of trouble for a whole day.

Tutor time

Your form tutor is telling you the pea soup joke again, when she notices you're wearing sunglasses. Sunglasses are against uniform rules. Do you:

A Say you need them on account of her dazzling wit, and keep them on.

B Apologise and put them in your bag.

Lesson 1

You have absolutely no idea what Monsieur Français is talking about. Do you:

A Make him stop by pretending to pass out.

B Ask him to explain.

Lesson 2

History – great! But Andy Payne (he's A. Pain!) on the desk behind you keeps prodding your shoulder. Do you:

A Break his stupid arm.

B Glare at him until he gets the message.

Break

You've forgotten to bring a snack and there's an ice cream van on the road beyond the playing fields, which is out of bounds. Do you:

A Try and climb over the fence to get a choc ice.
B Settle for some crisps from the school shop.

Lesson 3

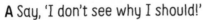

You haven't done your maths homework. Do you:

A Say, 'I don't see why I should!'
B Make an excuse and promise to do it tonight.

Lunch

Your mum's made you beetroot sandwiches. Do you:

A Pinch someone else's.
B Impress your mates with your vampire teeth.

Lesson 4

It's science with Mr 'Cough' McClone, and you're losing the will to live. Do you liven things up by:

A Playing games on your phone.
B Secretly counting how many times he coughs.

Lesson 5

Your food tech teacher's in a stress because you've got more cake mix on the table than in the tins. Do you:

A Shout back, with hand gestures.
B Clean it up.

Detentions

Being given a detention is actually just a fancy name for being kept in at break time/lunch time/after school. Sometimes you're given extra work to do; sometimes you have a task, such as picking up litter.

You usually get a verbal warning first, so you have a chance to avoid getting a detention by simply stopping being a pain. Your head of year has to notify your parents before keeping you in after school.

Occasionally, you might get a whole-class detention, especially if your teacher is having a bad day. You might not think it's unfair but then, life isn't fair. The best thing to do is just suck it up and get over it, unless it happens a lot. In that case, you should speak to your form tutor or head of year, as Class 7G did.

Class 7G and the three Olivers

There were three noisy trouble-makers in 7G, and they were all called Oliver. They messed about in every lesson, and none of the teachers could control them. Pretty soon, 7G had a reputation as the noisiest class in the school, and they were always getting class detentions.

At the end of one really bad week, when the class had missed virtually every break time, some of the kids went to see their form tutor. They showed her a list of all the detentions they had had that week, and explained that they felt pretty upset and annoyed at being labelled a bad class.

The form tutor told them that the teachers didn't think the whole class was bad – the idea of a class detention was to get the well-behaved kids to put pressure on the disruptive ones to stop.

'But that isn't fair,' the kids said. 'Why should we be punished for what the Olivers are doing?' The form tutor agreed. She said she was sure that the subject teachers didn't realise they were all giving class detentions. From then on, the class detentions stopped, and it was only the Olivers who missed out on their break times.

Other sanctions

If detentions don't cure you of your evil ways, secondary schools have a range of other sanctions they can impose on you. These include:

1 Getting parents involved

In the first instance, the school will phone your parents. If your teachers decide that your behaviour is still not improving, your parents may be asked to attend a meeting with senior staff at your school. This is often embarrassing enough to do the trick but, if it doesn't, they may be called in again.

2 Being put on report

If you keep being disruptive you can be put on report. This means you will be given set targets for better behaviour and a timescale to meet them.

3 The sanctions room

A lot of secondary schools have a sanctions room, where you have to sit on your own at a desk and do work set by your subject teachers in absolute silence. You could be sent there to cool off if you are being so disruptive that everyone else needs a break and you have ignored a verbal warning. You may have to spend a whole day or more in the sanctions room if you keep disrupting lessons.

4 Exclusion

If things still haven't improved, the school can exclude you for a fixed period. Kids can be permanently excluded from school for the sake of the rest of the students and staff, but only as a last resort. Exclusion can be used after a single incident if you do something really bad.

You – not u!

'U' might always be in trouble, but you don't have to be. Secondary school rules are as easy as ABCDE, so you aren't likely to break any by mistake. They are there to create a safe and pleasant environment, not to scare everyone witless, and if you have a positive attitude towards them, a verbal warning is probably the worst sanction you'll ever get.

10 No worries!

Going up to secondary school is a great adventure. Like going on safari, it involves:

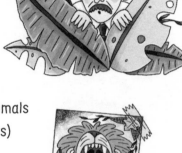

- getting the right equipment
- entering unfamiliar territory
- teaming up with new people
- not antagonising the wild animals (some older kids and teachers)
- learning new skills
- keeping out of trouble.

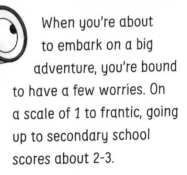

When you're about to embark on a big adventure, you're bound to have a few worries. On a scale of 1 to frantic, going up to secondary school scores about 2-3.

The scale of one to frantic

GET A LIFE ZONE

1 *Niggles, 'What if...'*
For example, 'What if they cancel The Simpsons because of the rugby?'

INFORMATION ZONE

2 *Wonders, 'What if...'*
For example, 'What if I've got the wrong stuff?'

3 *Worries, 'What if...'*
For example, 'No, really – what if I've got the wrong stuff?'

THERAPY ZONE

4 *Obsesses, 'What if...'*
For example, 'What if I've got the wrong stuff?' What if I've got the wrong stuff? What if I've got the wrong stuff...' etc.

PANIC ZONE

5 *Frantic – beyond 'What if...'*
For example, being chased down the road by three big, mean dogs.

As you can see, 2-3 is the information zone; worries here can be sorted out by simply getting information. All the information you need is in this book. But have you clocked it? Do the Going Up To Secondary test, and see.

 ## GUTS Test

At secondary school...

1 It's best to ignore the uniform and wear pink socks.

Agree / disagree / don't know

2 Only idiots get lost.

Agree / disagree / don't know

3 All the other new kids are keen to make new friends.

Agree / disagree / don't know

4 You have to show the bigger kids how hard you are, by blocking up the sinks in the toilets, etc.

Agree / disagree / don't know

5 All the teachers love it when you lark around.

Agree / disagree / don't know

6 The work's so difficult, even Einstein couldn't do it.

Agree / disagree / don't know

7 You can make homework work for you.

Agree / disagree / don't know

8 The rules are specially designed to catch you out.

Agree / disagree / don't know

RESULTS

If you've got any 'don't knows' - You don't know? Go back and read this book again!

If you disagree with 3 and 7 and agree with the rest – You're having a laugh, right? You're ready to go up.

If you agree with 3 and 7, and disagree with the rest – You're ready to go up – no worries!

So it's goodbye to primary school...

Your primary school will probably organise some events that are designed to help you celebrate and say goodbye to that stage of your life. These might include:

- a special leavers' assembly
- making a yearbook

- a class trip or outing
- a party or disco
- a leavers' photograph
- a performance for parents and younger pupils.

Here are three things you can do for yourself:

1. Buy a small gift or card for your class teacher to say thank you for all their help over the last year. Ditto for your headteacher.

2. Give a card or letter to any other teachers or helpers you have particularly enjoyed having at primary school. Tell them what you liked about them.

3. Have a picnic/barbecue/party with your mates from primary to celebrate all the fun times you've had there together.

Endings can be sad times, but if you keep looking back you can't see where you're going. Marking the end of primary school with gifts and parties is a way of helping you to move on.

And it's hello to secondary!

Your secondary school will probably organise events for you before you go up, such as activity days, social evenings and visits. These are designed to make sure you don't feel anxious about going up. They are also meant to give you a taster of some of the great things that secondary schools have to offer.

You're going to have heaps of new opportunities at secondary school. So what are your hopes and dreams for your time there? Are you a budding actor, who can't wait to get up on the stage? Or a brilliant footballer, just burning to get out on the field? Do you love painting and want to have your own exhibition one day? Or do you just want to meet loads of new people, and have fun?

 Do you want to be a genius, or join a pop group, or make a video? You're about to have all the facilities you need to set you on your way.

Deciding what you want is the first step towards making it happen. Make a 'wishes collage' to see (quite literally) what you want to get from secondary school.

THE **WISHES** COLLAGE

You will need
A few old magazines, a glue stick, some scissors and a large piece of paper (stick two small pieces together if you haven't got a large one).

What to do
1. Spend five minutes flicking through the magazines, tearing out anything that appeals to you, while you're thinking about what you hope to find at secondary school. These might include colours or patterns that feel right, plus people, scenes, objects and words. Don't think too much about it – just do it.
2. Cut or tear the pictures down to size and stick them on the large piece of paper.
3. Put it on your wall.

Make as many wishes collages as you like. Enjoy your dreams. New beginnings can be scary, but they're exciting too. Focusing on your hopes is a great way of keeping your fears in perspective.

Information is like warm socks...

... it's a great cure for cold feet!

All the information that you need about going up to secondary school is in this book. So if anything's still bugging you...

... you know what to do!